**because
two are
better
than one**

for you, friend

Nancy

with love,

Pat

date

12-25-04

Our purpose at Howard Publishing is to:

- *Increase faith* in the hearts of growing Christians
- *Inspire holiness* in the lives of believers
- *Instill hope* in the hearts of struggling people everywhere

Because He's coming again!

You and Me, Friend © 2004 by Philis Boultinghouse
All rights reserved. Printed in Mexico
Published by Howard Publishing Co., Inc.
3117 North 7th Street, West Monroe, LA 71291-2227

04 05 06 07 08 09 10 11 12 13   10 9 8 7 6 5 4 3 2 1

Edited by Between the Lines
Interior design by LinDee Loveland and Stephanie D. Walker

ISBN: 1-58229-380-5

Scriptures taken from the HOLY BIBLE, NEW INTERNATIONAL VERSION ®. Copyright © 1973, 1978, 1984 by International Bible Society. Used by permission of Zondervan Publishing House. All rights reserved.

because two are better than one

you
and
me
friend

HOWARD
PUBLISHING CO.

Printed in Mexico

Philis Boultinghouse

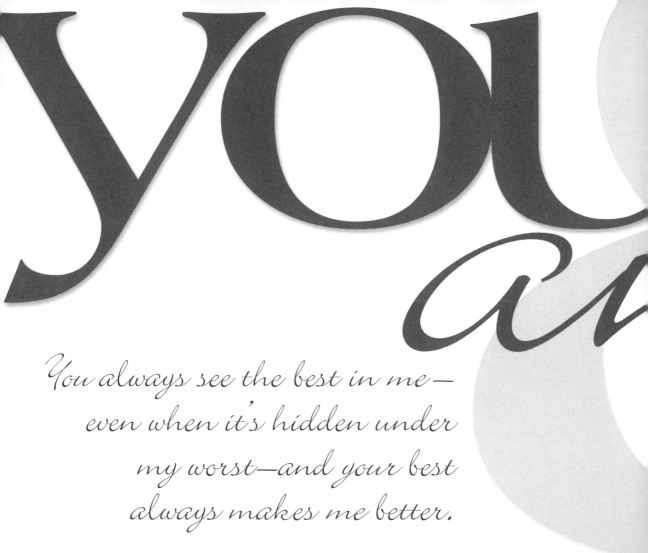

You always see the best in me—
even when it's hidden under
my worst—and your best
always makes me better.

Friend

In the sweetness of friendship
let there be laughter,
and sharing of pleasures.

Kahlil Gibran

Ballerina Buddies

June was alone. She shifted uncomfortably in the vinyl waiting-room chair and glanced at the clock. 11:15. Only two minutes since she'd last checked. Why she was still here she didn't know. Her father was in intensive care after heart surgery, and the night-shift nurse had told her she wouldn't be allowed back into his room until morning. The Muzak tunes playing in the background crept into her consciousness as a familiar melody took her back in time . . .

∾

June was alone. She sat on a folding chair in the old gymnasium and glanced at the clock. 9:15. Only two minutes since she'd last checked. She was thirteen, and it was her first school dance. Why they called it a dance she didn't know. No one was dancing. The giggly girls huddled along one wall, and the boys stood awkwardly, hands in their pockets, along another. But neither group seemed to notice June.

It was then that she heard that infectious laugh for the first time. A girl with dark red hair and matching freckles burst into the room. The exuberant redhead carried herself with a confident cheerfulness in spite of her gawky appearance. She was tall and skinny and seemed to be all arms and legs. She moved with such a lack of grace that each step seemed a precursor to catastrophe. But she appeared totally unaware of her clumsiness and fully delighted with life.

Her happy manner made June feel even more alone. To avoid simply sitting there, June decided to go to the punch table. She slid along the walls, trying to remain unnoticed. It was just 9:25. Her father wouldn't be picking her up until 10:30. She lowered her head and started back to her chair. She'd gone just a few steps when a flurry of arms and legs plowed into her. Her plastic punch cup flew into the air, spilling pink punch on her yellow dress. Her assailant let out a shrill yelp and then exploded into laughter. It was the gangly redhead.

"Oh, I'm so sorry! I didn't even notice you," the girl said, laughter punctuating every syllable. "I've made a horrible mess of your dress. And look at me! I'm just as bad. Come on! Let's go to the rest room and clean up."

Without waiting for a reply, the girl looped her arm through June's and dragged her toward the rest room. Once inside, she erupted into laughter again. "I can't believe I ran into you like that. I'm such a klutz!"

June could only stare at the bubbly girl in front of her.

"What a nincompoop I am! I spilled punch all over you, dragged you in here, and I haven't even told you my name. I'm Kris—Kris Kreech. What's your name?"

"My—my name is June."

"I like that name," Kris announced. "It's summery and sounds fun. Look, June," she continued, gesturing toward their stained dresses, "this is hopeless. We can't go back out there looking like this."

June nodded in agreement, horrified at the thought of being the object of such unflattering attention.

"My older sister is with me." Kris rolled her eyes dramatically. "Mom sent her to chaperone. She can drive us to my house, and we can get out of these clothes and into something comfortable. I'm sure I can find something to fit you."

"Oh, no, I couldn't do that," June protested. "I'll call my dad to pick me up."

"Oh, come on. It'll be fun. I just moved here, and I don't know a soul. I came to this dance with my older sister. How lame is that!"

"Well, I came alone," June confessed before she knew it, feeling more comfortable with this stranger than she did with the other girls, whom she had known from a distance for years.

"You can call your parents from my house and let them know where you are," Kris said. She took June by the elbow and led her to the door.

Before June knew it, she was in the backseat of the Kreech car, chatting away as though she'd known Kris all her life. When they got to Kris's house, Mrs. Kreech called June's father and told him what had happened. "Can June stay for a while? The girls can watch a movie and turn this little mishap into a fun evening."

June could tell that Mrs. Kreech's friendly assurances convinced her father to let her stay.

As Kris searched for clothes that would fit her guest, June surveyed Kris's bedroom. It was decorated in the same haphazard, exuberant style Kris radiated. But one item stood out from the rest. Its delicacy and elegance was an obvious contrast to the rest of the room. June picked up the beautiful music box and opened the lid. Not one, but two ballerinas popped up and began twirling to a tune she recognized immediately from her old piano lessons: "You'll Never Walk Alone."

"My aunt Elizabeth gave that to me. She said the music

reminded her of my laughter, and the ballerina symbolized the grace that's hidden inside me." Kris laughed again. "Everyone knows I don't have any grace on the outside; my family's hoping there's some on the inside. Aunt Elizabeth says she already sees it. She's my favorite aunt."

"Why are there two ballerinas?" June asked, enthralled. "Most music boxes have only one."

"Aunt Elizabeth says one is me and the other is my soul mate—a friend I'll meet someday who will see the grace hidden in me. I know it's silly, but that's my aunt Elizabeth."

June carefully set the music box back on the dresser. "I don't have any aunts," she said wistfully. "And my mother died when I was ten. Dad doesn't know much about hidden grace or ballerinas—or any other girl stuff."

"Hey," Kris said. "My aunt Elizabeth is coming to visit next week. Maybe you could meet her . . . "

~

The harsh ring of a phone in the waiting room jarred June out of her reverie. A glance toward the clock told her it was almost midnight. She was exhausted and depressed. There was no need for her to stay, but somehow she just couldn't go. Her father was all the family she had. *What if something went wrong? What if there were complications from the surgery? What if he died and left her all alone?*

Trying to shake off her gloomy mood, June picked up her Styrofoam cup of cold coffee and headed for the hospitality room and some fresh coffee. As she rounded the corner, someone plowed into her. Her coffee cup flew into the air, spilling the dark liquid down the front of her yellow silk suit. The eruption of laughter told her immediately that Kris Kreech had struck again.

"I'm so sorry," Kris said through her giggles. "I am the perpetual klutz. I don't think I'll ever outgrow it!"

"What are you doing here? It's almost midnight!"

"You've been on my mind all day, but Maggie's been sick with an ear infection, and I just got her to sleep. Jay promised to listen for her while I came to see you. I knew I'd find you here. How's your dad?"

"The doctor said that he came through the surgery fine and would sleep through the night, but for some reason I just can't leave. Nervous, I guess . . . or afraid."

"Let's sit down for a minute," Kris said gently. "I've got something for you."

Only then did June notice the brightly colored gift bag overflowing with shredded yellow tissue paper. Kris led her to a couch in the hospitality room and extended the bag. "In the spirit of Aunt Elizabeth," she said with a twinkle in her green eyes.

"What in the world . . . ?" June pushed the tissue paper aside and reached into the bag. As she pulled out the gift, what she saw took her breath away. It was the exquisite music box from Kris's childhood room. She opened the lid, as she had done so many times before, and the twin ballerinas popped up and began their dance.

"You can't give me this," June protested. "It was a gift from your aunt."

"You, June, are the fulfillment of Aunt Elizabeth's prediction. You've become my best friend—my soul mate—and you have always seen the grace hidden in me. You have the eyes of a true friend—you look beyond my awkward exterior and see into my heart. You are who Aunt Elizabeth had in mind when she bought this gift for me—my ballerina buddy."

June's eyes filled with tears, and she wrapped her arms around her friend. "When I felt unnoticed and all alone, you plowed into my life and became my friend. I know I'll never be alone as long as you're around." June turned her teary eyes to the twirling ballerinas. "It's you and me, friend—ballerina buddies forever."

Ten Things My Friend and I Have Given Each Other as Gifts

1 *A music box*

2 *A mulberry-scented candle*

3 *Bubble bath*

4 *A box of chocolates*

5 *Flowers*

6 *A handmade Raggedy Ann doll*

7 *A tennis outfit*

8 *A personally crocheted baby blanket*

9 *A door wreath*

10 *A lifetime of memories*

thank

you...

*for seeing who I want to be
instead of who I am.*

Double Vision

She's got double vision. It's really kind of odd. She knows the truth about me, yet she makes me feel as if I'm a quality person, anyway. She knows I can sometimes be overbearing, and she's heard me say some really dumb things. But her heart sees my heart, and she senses my intentions and gives me the benefit of the doubt.

Like the time her little boy had his tonsils removed and I forgot because I was caught up in my own agenda. She believed me when I said I was sorry, and she didn't hold it against me. Or the day I shot off my mouth and tried to tell her how to handle something in her life that I knew nothing about. She gave me her "I love you, but I'm going to have to hurt you if you don't shut up" look. Once again I had to say I was sorry, and she hugged me and said she knew the better part of me.

Then there was the time I hurt her feelings—and I didn't say I was sorry. She was the one who made the first move. She came to me and told me that the words that had come out of my mouth didn't sound like the me she knew.

It's like I said. She's got double vision. She sees who I want to be more than who I am. How blessed I am to have such a friend.

I thank my God every time I

remember you. In all my prayers

for all of you, I always pray with

joy because of your partnership in

the gospel from the first day until

now, being confident of this, that

he who began a good work in you

will carry it on to completion until

the day of Christ Jesus.

—Philippians 1:3–6

Dearest friend,

Whenever I think of you, I thank God. Just knowing you has filled my life with joy. You have the amazing quality of seeing me as the person I want to be instead of who I really am. You see me as the finished person I hope to someday be. I thank God for you.

Your thankful friend

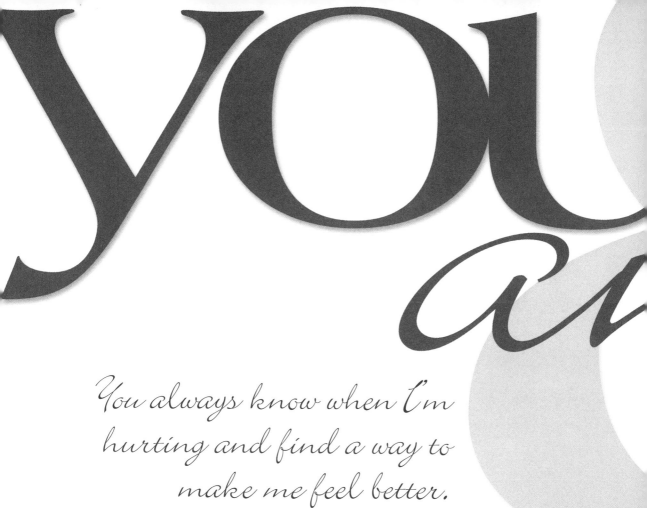

You always know when I'm hurting and find a way to make me feel better.

Friend

A friend is one
who walks in
when others walk out.

Walter Winchell

Flowers for Marcie

Marcie sat in her office, head cradled in her hands. The wave of emotion had hit her hard—unexpectedly. Large, silent tears slid down her cheeks. How would she make it through this day?

As if on cue, Stephanie appeared at Marcie's office door. She hurried to her friend and knelt by her side. Stroking Marcie's hair gently, she tried to find her friend's eyes. "Hey, birthday girl, what's wrong? You're not *that* old. After all, you're a year younger than I am—you'll always be young in my book."

Marcie tried to meet her friend's eyes with a brave smile, but when she saw the compassion in her eyes, she dissolved into tears again.

"I was thinking about Allen," she said between sobs. "This is my first birthday without him. He always did this special thing . . . and, well . . . I miss him." Marcie attempted to pull herself together.

"I'm just being whiny. I've got way too much work to do to carry on like this."

"You are not being whiny. You expect too much of yourself, Marcie. As tough as you are, you're not superwoman."

Marcie managed a mirthless smile. "I know, but I've got to be strong. I can't fall apart today just because it's my birthday. I'll be OK."

"Sure you will," Stephanie assured her. "But you don't have to be strong with me. I'm your friend, remember? Look, in thirty minutes it'll be time for lunch—and I promised to treat you for your birthday."

"I haven't forgotten," Marcie said, the first hint of a real smile on her face. "Thanks."

Marcie turned back to her computer and her many unanswered e-mails. But she couldn't focus. The words swam as her eyes teared up again. Her thoughts returned to that day—more than thirty years ago—when Aunt Margaret had said the words she would never forget.

"Marcie, Allen . . . I have to tell you something." Marcie remembered her aunt's hands shaking and her face twisting in a way that scared her. "Your mommy and daddy . . . " Aunt Margaret's words had been choked by her sobs. Though just six, Marcie instantly understood that her life would never be the same. "Your mommy and daddy were in a car accident. Oh, sweeties, they're gone. Your mommy and daddy were killed."

Before Marcie or Allen could react, Aunt Margaret had gathered them in her arms and squeezed them so tightly that four-year-old Allen cried from the squeezing. Allen and Marcie had sat stiffly in her embrace, unable to take in the reality of what their aunt had told them.

Marcie grabbed a tissue and tried to dry her eyes. But the tears just wouldn't stop. Aunt Margaret and Uncle James had raised her and Allen as their own children. But Marcie had been right—their lives never were the same.

Marcie had done everything she could to be strong for Allen—but she was just a little girl. It was the little things that hurt most, like remembering her father's tradition of giving her roses for her birthday, one for every year. The first time—her fourth birthday—Daddy had come home with four roses, each a different color. Mommy had put them in a white vase and set them on Marcie's dresser. She had been thrilled to have her very own flowers. They were just like the flowers Daddy gave Mommy for her birthday. Best of all, she got to smell and touch them all she wanted.

He'd done the same thing on her fifth and sixth birthdays. No matter what other gifts she got, the roses from her daddy were always her favorite.

On her seventh birthday—the first without her parents—Marcie had cried the whole morning. When Aunt Margaret asked what was wrong, Marcie just cried harder. She ran to her room and flung herself across her bed, aching for the white vase filled with colorful roses on her very own dresser.

Only when Allen came into her room did her sobbing slow. She had to be strong for her little brother. Allen had padded over to the bed and sat beside her. He put his hand on her back and whispered, "Marcie, please tell me what's wrong."

Marcie dried her tears and pulled herself to a sitting position. She took Allen's hand in hers. "Allen, I'm crying because I miss Mommy and Daddy—especially today because it's my birthday. Daddy used to bring me roses—one for each year old I was." She had smiled at the memory. "He'd get as many colors as he could find. Today he would have brought me seven roses. Mommy would have put them in a white vase in my room so I could touch and smell them all I wanted." She sniffled. "I miss that. Do you understand?"

Allen had nodded somberly and laid his head on Marcie's shoulder.

Grown-up Marcie forced herself to read the e-mail on her screen.

As project manager for a busy design firm, she never seemed to catch up. But halfway through her first memo, Marcie's mind returned to her seventh birthday.

Aunt Margaret had invited Marcie's friends to a party for her and had bought her a Barbie cake like her friend Alice had had for her birthday. The cake formed Barbie's skirt—it was even more beautiful than her friend Alice's cake had been. Marcie had gotten every present she'd asked for and then some. But after the cake was eaten, the friends had gone home, and the presents were put away, Marcie had gone to her room and closed the door. She'd gotten everything but the one thing she wanted most.

That was when she'd heard a knock on her door, and Allen had come in with his hand behind his back. "I got you a present, Marcie— like Daddy." With that, he'd held out a fistful of flowers—seven in all. Some were weeds from the field behind Aunt Margaret's house, and some were flowers from neighbors' yards. "I couldn't find any roses,"

Allen had said cautiously, "but they're all different colors. Maybe Aunt Margaret will let us use one of her flower holders."

"They're perfect!" Marcie had squealed. "This is my favorite present of all!"

She would never forget Allen's beaming face. After that, Allen had always given her flowers for her birthday—one for every year and as many different colors as he could find. As he'd gotten older and had money of his own, he'd started buying roses—just like their dad.

On the eve of her last birthday, Stephanie had helped Allen get into her office after hours and fill it with forty-one roses—in every available color—in big, white vases. When she'd come into her office on her birthday, she'd been greeted by their sweet fragrance and beauty.

But three months after that birthday, Aunt Margaret had once again been the bearer of bad news. Allen had been killed in a convenience-store robbery. He'd been at the wrong place at the wrong time. Now he was gone—the last member of her immediate family, her last real link to Mom and Dad.

Marcie was jolted back to the present when Stephanie stuck her head in the door. "Hey, girl, it's time to go! Ready?"

At the restaurant, the hostess led the two friends through rows of tables to a back room. As they entered, a loud "Surprise!" stopped Marcie in her tracks. All her coworkers were gathered around a festive table with a beautifully decorated cake in the center. Beside the cake were several gifts. Marcie was truly pleased at the thoughtfulness of her friends and colleagues.

As they walked back into the office building, Marcie hugged Stephanie. "Thank you for the wonderful surprise; it was just what I needed."

"I'm so glad," Stephanie replied with a squeeze. "Enjoy the rest of your day."

As Marcie approached her office door, a familiar fragrance filled the air. It was the smell of her father, the smell of her brother; it was the smell of roses. She opened the door and was greeted with a visual delight. White vases filled with roses were everywhere. Two huge arrangements were on her desk, three more on her credenza. Every shelf, every corner—*everywhere*—overflowed with roses of every color and variety.

"There are 126 roses," Stephanie said from behind her. "Forty-two from your mom, forty-two from Allen, and forty-two from your dad. Happy birthday, sweetie. Your friends love you very much.

"And one more thing: You can smell and touch them all you want."

Ten Things My Friend and I Like to Do Together

1 *Go antique shopping*

2 *Eat malted milk balls*

3 *Take a walk— especially in a park*

4 *Watch videos*

5 *Go to the beach*

6 *Eat lunch at a "girlie" restaurant*

7 *Pile all our kids in the Suburban and go to the water park*

8 *Talk about our kids*

9 *Talk about our husbands (lovingly, of course)*

10 *Share our most outrageous dreams for the future*

thank

you...

*for always being there
when I need you.*

A Friend You Can Count On

No matter how busy our lives get—even when they're going in opposite directions—I can always count on my friend to be there when I need her. Like the Sunday morning after I'd stayed up all night waiting on a daughter who didn't come home. My friend called, and when she heard the fear in my voice, she came to sit by my side. She didn't have any magic words or instant solutions, but she came . . . and she sat . . . and she cried with me.

She's not only there for the big things; she's there for the little things too. She'll pick up a gallon of milk for me when she goes to the store or a gift for the bridal shower I forgot to shop for. She'll run an errand for me when her day is even busier than mine, and she'll lend her party-planning talents to arrange a surprise party for my husband or my mother-in-law.

I can count on her. That's what it boils down to. I know, without a doubt, that if I need her, she'll be there. I'm not as good at it as she is, but because of her, I'm getting better. She helps me be a better friend. She helps me be more others-centered, more aware of how I can offer myself to make someone else's day a little easier. Watching her, I've become more of a servant, more dependable—someone others can count on to be there when they need a friend.

We who are strong ought to bear

with the failings of the weak and

not to please ourselves. Each of us

should please his neighbor for his

good, to build him up.

—Romans 15:1–2

Dear friend,

How is it that you know when I need your strength? It seems that when I am at my weakest, you become strong for me. Your very presence calms my fears and reminds me to hope. You're always thinking of how you can make my life easier. Thank you for sharing your strength with me.

Your indebted friend

It takes time to grow a friend.
Laughter, pain, and days on end,
Movies, picnics, camping trips—
These are things that grow friendships.

It takes love to grow a friend.
Forgiveness so that hurts can mend,
Looking to the other's needs,
Often doing thoughtful deeds.

It takes trust to grow a friend.
Secrets not thrown to the wind,
Words are kept with tender care,
Treasured as a gift most rare.

It takes hope to grow a friend.
Belief that friendship never ends,
Vision for a future day,
Friends forever, come what may.

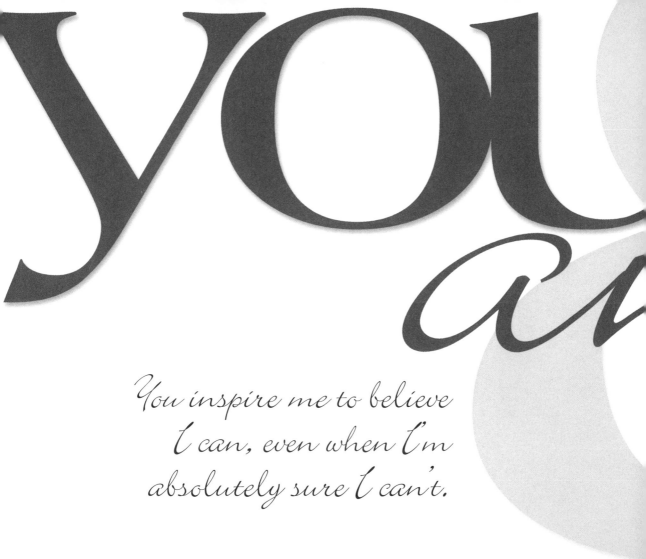

you a

You inspire me to believe
I can, even when I'm
absolutely sure I can't.

Feelings are
the connective tissue
of friendship.

Joel D. Block

Butterflies

"I want to feel butterflies," Tessa said earnestly. "Does that sound ridiculously romantic?" She lifted her eyes tentatively to meet the puzzled gaze of her friend.

Alesa stood beside Tessa, pouring her a second cup of coffee. After setting a plate of muffins on her kitchen table, Alesa slid into the chair across from her friend.

"Butterflies?" she asked quizzically. "What do you mean?"

Tessa wasn't sure she should continue, but the encouragement and concern in Alesa's expression made her feel safe.

"You know—that fluttery feeling in your stomach when the guy you like walks into the room. Or even that queasy feeling when you're in sixth grade and you walk out on stage to say your lines in the school play. Whether it's puppy love or nervous jitters, those butterflies let you know you're alive."

Understanding spread across Alesa's face as she cradled her coffee cup in her hands and put it to her lips. "I know what you mean," she said knowingly. "I remember my first date with Joe. I was so nervous. I spent hours on my hair and makeup. When I finally heard the doorbell ring, my stomach filled with butterflies. I thought I was going to be sick!" She chuckled at the memory. "We've been married ten years, and I still—" she stopped abruptly and reached across the table to touch Tessa's hand. "I'm sorry, Tessa, I didn't mean to go on about me and Joe like that."

"Don't apologize," Tessa protested. "Just because I'm feeling bad doesn't mean you should be miserable. Anyway, butterflies really aren't all they're cracked up to be." Tessa's pensive moment had passed. "I'm better off sticking to more practical things—like paying the bills and helping the kids with their homework. This butterfly talk is really just girlish fantasy. I'm a grown woman with serious responsibilities."

Since her husband left her nine months ago for his attractive, young secretary, Tessa had gone from a comfortable lifestyle as a stay-at-home mom to breadwinner and single parent of two rambunctious boys.

Sure, Rick helped out a little with child support. But even after Tessa and Rick had split the money from the sale of their beautiful home, and she and the boys had moved into a small apartment, she always ran out of money before she ran out of month. With a full-time job and full-time responsibilities at home, Tessa usually felt overwhelmed, exhausted, and depressed. She certainly had *not* felt any butterflies . . . not in a very long time.

"Butterflies are for schoolgirls," Tessa said with a decided resignation in her voice. "They're fragile and easily broken, and I've got to be strong. I don't have time for foolish daydreams. I've got to pick up the boys in fifteen minutes."

"Tessa, don't give up your butterfly dream," Alesa urged her. "It's OK to dream. You don't have to be practical all the time. I'm certain there'll be butterflies in your future."

"Experience tells me otherwise," Tessa dismissed her. "I have too many real-life concerns to get distracted by dreams of butterflies. I've got to get going."

As she drove away, Tessa remembered the butterflies she used to feel when Rick walked into a room. But that was a lifetime ago. Would she ever feel that alive again? Tessa shook her head to bring herself back to the life she lived now—a life devoid of butterflies and romance.

Routine filled Tessa's days. Thoughts of butterflies and other fantasies were crushed by the heavy sadness that ruled her heart. One evening, after she'd finally gotten the boys to sleep after a particularly difficult day, she collapsed into the sagging La-Z Boy and dissolved into tears.

This is too much, she thought. *I can't do all of this by myself. Rick and his new wife are probably enjoying a romantic evening in their new house, and here I sit all alone in this crummy apartment.*

The sharp ring of the phone interrupted Tessa's misery. She gathered her composure and tried to sound normal as she answered it. But before she could say anything, Alesa's cheerful voice chirped, "Hey there, friend. How are you?"

At the warm sound of her friend's voice, Tessa lost all resolve to hold it together and melted into tears once again. "I'm not doing so well," she admitted. "I don't know if I can do this, Alesa. It's too much. With the boys and work and keeping up the apartment—I just can't do it all. The worst part is feeling so alone," she confided. "After all Rick has done, I still love him."

"Listen, girl, how about going shopping with me Saturday morning? Maybe your mom can keep the boys."

"I guess that sounds OK. She did offer to take the boys to the park to give me a break."

"Great. I'll pick you up around nine. We can shop for a while, then stop at that little coffee shop for some cappuccino and muffins."

Alesa picked Tessa up at nine sharp. They dropped the boys at Tessa's mom's, then headed for a brief retreat from chaos. But instead of heading for their favorite shopping center, Alesa turned onto the Interstate.

"Where are you going?" Tessa asked.

"I'm taking you on a little distraction."

"I don't have time for a distraction," Tessa protested. "I have to get the boys at eleven."

"That's what you think. Everything's taken care of. Your mom will keep the boys until three, then Joe will pick them up and take them to our house to play with Sarah and Mattie. Just sit back and relax, Tess. We're going to one of my favorite places. Santa Cruz is just a couple of hours from here, and there's a great beach with a beautiful lighthouse. You'll love it."

"Sounds like I don't have any choice in the matter," Tessa said, feigning grumpiness.

"You're right. You don't," Alesa confirmed.

Tessa began to relax as she settled back for the pleasant drive. Although it was a cold November day, the California sun was shining, and Alesa put in a CD of Tessa's favorite classical music. The two friends shared stories of the latest cute things their children had said and the mischief they'd gotten into. Alesa made a couple of attempts at stirring Tessa's hopes for a brighter future, but Tessa always steered the conversation to the past or present. The future was too daunting.

As they neared the coastline, Tessa caught a glimpse of the light-house. The view was spectacular. When they stopped, Tessa opened the car door and stepped out, mesmerized by the sight before her. A beautifully kept, white lookout tower topped a sturdy, red-brick structure. The wind whipped through their hair as the two women walked into the field of wildflowers and tall, brown grass that lay between them and the lighthouse. As their feet stirred the purple flowers, another stirring caused Tessa to catch her breath. Hundreds of quivering butterflies rose from the undergrowth and filled the air. Their golden wings fluttered against the breeze. One flew so close it tickled Tessa's cheek.

"What . . . ?" Tessa started in amazement.

"They're butterflies—monarchs," Alesa explained. "They migrate here in the winter. Aren't they beautiful?"

Caught up in wonder, Tessa spread her arms and twirled in circles like a little girl, her face raised to the sky. "I feel butterflies," she squealed, "I really feel them!"

She continued spinning until she fell in a dizzy heap on the ground. Butterflies swirled around and above her, and she felt as though they were lifting her heavy heart on their wings.

"See?" Alesa said as she plopped down to join her. "Don't abandon your dream. Look for the butterflies. They may seem fragile, but these butterflies were strong enough to fly all the way from the Rocky Mountains to get to warmer country. You have that same strength in you."

For the first time since Rick had left, Tessa felt a glimmer of hope and strength. As she watched the monarchs flit from flower to flower, the peace she once knew began to grow in her heart again.

"Alesa, you are an amazing friend. You'll never know what you've done for me today. You've given me a vision for the future—a future where I'll not only feel butterflies, but where I can be one too."

Tessa lifted her face to the sunshine and breathed in the fresh, clean air. She knew there'd be many rough days ahead, but she also knew that today she had turned a corner. She felt truly alive for the first time in months. Things would be different now. She was going to make it after all.

Ten Emotions My Friend and I Have Shared

1 *Joy*

2 *Grief*

3 *Anger*

4 *Peace*

5 *Sadness*

6 *Elation*

7 *Regret*

8 *Sorrow*

9 *Anticipation*

10 *Love*

thank

you....

for allowing me to call you friend.
Your enthusiasm for life
makes me smile.

Zest for Life

She turned fifty just last month, but her zest for life matches that of any twenty-year-old—probably surpasses most. I got my first glimpse of her relentless vitality when she told me about her one hundred list. "List of what?" I asked. "A list of one hundred things I want to do before I die." On her list were things like learning to play tennis, memorizing the constellations, and seeing the Great Wall of China. Just last week she started taking tennis lessons one day a week after work. Mark that one off the list. What will be next?

Her enthusiasm isn't the result of a charmed life. Far from it. I've seen her maintain her smile and composure through the most trying circumstances—things I only learned about accidentally, because she's not one to put the spotlight on her woes. She carries herself with dignity and poise that belie the pain in her life.

And you should see how she loves her grandbaby. Now, I know every grandma loves her grandchildren, but it's so much fun to watch her love hers. She's a long-distance grandma, but she finds creative ways to stay close to her little doll.

Every trip is "wonderful," every special occasion is "the best"—and she really means it! She inspires me to rise above the grind of everyday life and find glee in its little pleasures.

Just being around her makes me smile. I'm proud to call her my friend.

Your love has given me great joy and

encouragement, because you . . .

have refreshed the hearts of the saints.

—Philemon 1:7

Hi friend,

Have you ever noticed that the word "courage" is hidden in the word "encouragement"? Whenever I feel alone or afraid, you have a way of saying just the right thing. And always hidden in your words of encouragement is a little bit of courage that goes straight to my heart.

Your encouraged friend

Your life is intertwined with
mine—the good and the bad.
I know we'll be friends forever.

I think there is a thread
that runs through each friendship
and keeps it going,
no words necessary.
Each knows what
the other knows about him,
through good times and bad.

Lauren Bacall

The Queen Bee Quilters

Twelve women sat around the quilting frame, threaded needles in hand—busily . . . rhythmically . . . precisely—stitching along their assigned paths. Opal Mitchell sat where she always did. Charlotte sat to her right, Marilyn to her left. The rest of the Queen Bee Quilters extended around the circle. Every Tuesday morning at ten they gathered together to quilt and talk. They'd been together—quilting and talking—for more than ten years.

Opal looked around the circle fondly as she pulled her thread taut, preparing for the next stitch. These women had been by her side through all of life's major events.

Edith, who'd survived three husbands, had sat with her all night on the eve of her own husband's death. Opal and Harry had been married for fifty-three years when he lost his battle with bone cancer. That was eight years ago, and she still reached for him in the night.

Then there was Margaret, whom she'd known since they were fifteen—back in the days when unmarried, pregnant girls were whisked away to live with distant aunts until the baby was born and given up for adoption. Margaret had kept Opal's secret to this day.

"Opal! Land sakes!" Marilyn scolded. "Look at your stitches. Your line looks like a winding country road. Where's your mind, old woman?"

Leave it to Marilyn to point out my blunders, Opal thought. But Marilyn was right. Her mind had wandered, and so had her stitches. "Drat!" Opal grumbled. "Now I'll have to redo that whole line. It's your fault, Marilyn. If you didn't keep bumping me every time you pull your stitch . . . " But the twinkle in Opal's eyes belied her words, and Marilyn smiled back.

"The only reason *you* keep bumping *me*," Marilyn retorted, "is that you keep scooting closer so you can learn the secret to my perfect stitch."

The women giggled and elbowed each other as Opal pulled out her crooked stitches.

"Who is this quilt going to?" Violet asked.

"It's for my granddaughter," Mary Jo replied, obviously perturbed that anyone would forget the wedding of her youngest grandchild. "Her bridal shower is three weeks away, and I want this to be perfect," she said with a sideways glance at Opal.

Mary Jo had started the Queen Bee tradition. She had always had a flamboyant sense of fashion, but with each passing year, she seemed to lose a bit more of her common sense and grow more outrageous in her style. Two years ago—just after Easter—Mary Jo had come to their quilting session wearing her Easter bonnet. It was a big straw hat with bright plastic flowers and a huge, blue satin bow. She'd even tucked a tacky bluebird amid the flowers. She said she'd gone to so much trouble to decorate it that it was silly to wear it just one day.

Her sister quilters knew Mary Jo was in the beginning stages of

Alzheimer's, so they'd gone along with her and told her it was pretty. Someone even said she looked like a queen. Elizabeth had asked if she could try it on, and then Mary Jo would not be satisfied until every one of them had worn it. Mary Jo had come up with the bright idea that each week they should take turns wearing it, and whoever wore it would be queen for the day.

Today it was Charlotte's turn, and she was milking her position for all it was worth. Ringing the bell that had become a queenly prop, Charlotte cleared her throat. "Marilyn, dear," she said with mock authority, "we desire another cookie."

"Get it yourself, you old—"

"Hast thou forgotten that I am your queen?" Charlotte reprimanded.

Apparently, Marilyn had forgotten. She rose to her feet, shoved her chair back noisily, and stomped over to the refreshment table. Stifled laughter followed her.

Opal looked around at her friends. She had told the group two months ago that her daughter and son-in-law were moving out of state and that she was going with them. She knew she'd made the right decision, but the thought of leaving this circle of women tore at her heart.

Not one person has said anything about this being my last week, she mused, disappointed. *How could they have forgotten?*

Opal fought back tears. Maybe she had misjudged the depth of their friendship. Maybe her leaving wasn't such a big deal after all. They certainly didn't seem to think so. *No one has said a single word . . .*

Opal's thoughts were interrupted by the ringing bell. "Ladies and devoted subjects," Charlotte announced, rising regally to her feet and standing behind Opal's chair. "May I have your attention, please?" She lifted the gaudy hat from her head and placed it on Opal's. "In honor of this auspicious—and very sad—occasion, I bequeath my crown to thee."

The tears Opal had been holding back began to flow, but they were tears of joy, not hurt.

"Ladies," Charlotte continued with affected authority, "assume your stations." Each woman picked up her chair and moved to form a circle. Charlotte and Marilyn turned Opal's chair so it was part of the circle.

"What's going on?" Opal protested.

"With all due respect, your majesty—put a cork in it! Sit there and chill; we have a presentation to make," Charlotte barked.

"Attendants!" she said. "Fetch the queen's present!" Marjorie and Edith disappeared into the storage closet and emerged with a box so big it took two of them to carry it. They placed it on Opal's lap, helping her balance it.

"We've put together a little something to show you what you mean to us," Charlotte said, blinking back tears. "Go ahead, open it."

Opal tore off the wrapping paper and took off the lid. She gasped. It was a quilt—lovingly made for her by her friends.

Marjorie and Edith lifted the quilt from the box and held it up for her to see. Charlotte stood by the quilt. "We've each made a square that represents one of the many things you've done for us, dear friend." She pointed to the square in the top left corner. A hand-stitched appliqué of a baby's cradle was encircled with embroidered stars.

"This square is in memory of the night you delivered my baby." Opal smiled and nodded, remembering. "I know you remember," Charlotte continued, "but not everyone has heard the story. Two weeks before my due date, at two in the morning, my water broke. It was my first baby, my husband was out of town, and I panicked. I didn't know you that well yet, but I knew you were a nurse, and I knew you and Harry had a car. The two of you were there within minutes after I called. We headed for the hospital in your old Chevrolet. Saying your car was old is putting it mildly. It broke down on a country road with no traffic and no one to help. I had that baby in the backseat! The conditions were less than ideal, but you made me feel safe and secure. I remember holding my baby in my arms and looking out the back window up at the stars. It's one of my most cherished memories. Thank you, my friend, for the impact you've had on my life—and my daughter's!"

Doris was next to stand. She pointed to her square and said, "My story isn't nearly as dramatic as Charlotte's, but your impact on my life was just as strong, Opal." Doris's square depicted a delicate teacup. "When I sent my last child off to college, I thought my life was over," she explained. "What purpose did I have? How would I fill my days without caring for a child? Opal, you sensed my pain and invited me over for a cup of tea. As we sat at your kitchen table, you encouraged me in two ways. First, you reminded me that I would always be Mother to my children. But beyond that, you gave me a vision for a new phase of life—a phase that was different but just as meaningful. Thank you, dear friend, for always encouraging my heart."

Each woman in the circle rose in turn and shared about the square she had made and how Opal had touched her life.

Finally, Margaret concluded: "These squares represent snapshots of your life, Opal. And what these snapshots show is that you've made deep impressions on the hearts of all of us. When we stitched all the squares together, we saw a beautiful portrait—a portrait of true friendship. And that's the significance of the center circle." In the center was a blue bonnet, and on the bonnet were embroidered the words *The Queen Bee Quilters—Friends for Life*.

Opal fingered the quilt tenderly, touched by the thought that each stitch had been placed there purposely, carefully, lovingly by her wonderful friends. Every stitch and every image was a picture of friendship— the kind of friendship that would last a lifetime.

Ten Things My Friend Has Forgotten

1 The time I forgot her birthday

2 The coffee stain I put on her favorite pink sweater

3 That I accidentally let slip a secret she had confided in me

4 That I broke the macaroni necklace her son made her for Mother's Day

5 That I got us lost on the way to her cousin's wedding

6 That I let all her houseplants die when she was on vacation

7 The day I was feeling so sorry for myself over a minor tragedy that I was oblivious to her deep pain

8 That I promised to pick up the cake for her husband's surprise thirtieth birthday party—but forgot

9 That I lost the top layer of her wedding cake she was saving for her first anniversary (Don't ask me how I lost it, but I did.)

10 The dent I put in her brand-new, red Mitsubishi convertible the third day she had it (Well, she hasn't totally forgotten that one.)

thank

you...

for remembering the things that
are important to me and
forgetting my mistakes.

A Friend Who Remembers

It's nice to have a friend who remembers you. Someone who, no matter what else is going on, remembers what's important to you. I have such a friend.

She remembers that I had a bad headache yesterday and calls to see how I'm doing. She remembers that my husband is out of town and invites me to go see a movie. She remembers my birthday. Not just the biggies—like when you turn thirty or forty—but the in-between ones too. Like thirty-eight. There's nothing special about turning thirty-eight, but she remembered.

She also remembers the anniversary of my brother's death and the fact that every time I hear the song "Peace Like a River," I think of him and cry. She remembers that I *love* chocolate—especially expensive, dark chocolate—and when she went to Switzerland, she bought three huge bars just for me. She remembered that my daughter was graduating from law school, and though she'd never met her, she bought a gift and sent it with me to her.

She remembers that I love to watch videos and eat malted milk balls. And every now and then, when her kids or mine are off visiting a grandma, we'll hole up in the childless house with stacks of movies and a couple of bags of the best malted milk balls and eat and laugh and cry until we can't stand it any more.

It's nice to have a friend who remembers.

Praise be to the God and Father

of our Lord Jesus Christ, the

Father of compassion and the

God of all comfort, who comforts

us in all our troubles, so that we

can comfort those in any trouble

with the comfort we ourselves

have received from God.

—2 Corinthians 1:3–4

Friend of mine,

What a comfort you are to me. When my life becomes heavy, you come along beside me and share the load. When I think I can't do it, you assure me that I can. When I get buried under the weight of too much to do, you help me dig my way out. You comfort my heart when it's weary. What a blessing you are to me.

Your grateful friend

Dearest heavenly Father,

You are the giver of all things good, so I know You've given my friend to me. She exhibits so many of Your marvelous characteristics. She is patient with me when I test her limits. She stands by my side when others melt away. She sees the best in me and inspires me to be even better. Thank You for this beautiful friend.

Father, help me to be a worthy friend in return. Grow in me the ability to focus on the good in her and barely be aware of her flaws. Teach me to be more thoughtful of her, to remember what's important to her, to rejoice when she rejoices and cry when she cries.

I ask Your most generous blessings on my dear friend. Fill her heart with Your peace and multiply her joy. Shower her and those she loves with safety and prosperity. Protect her, guide her, strengthen her, and bless her.

Amen